TREASURE

Uncovering Patterns
and Principles
That Create Prosperity

by Edwin Louis Cole

Southlake, Texas

*TREASURE: Uncovering Patterns and Principles
That Create Prosperity*

ISBN: 1-929496-07-9
Copyright © 2001 by Edwin Louis Cole
P. O. Box 10
Grapevine, TX 76099
www.edcole.org

Cover painting by Lyn Conlan
www.watercolorlyn.com

Published by Watercolor Books™
P. O. Box 93234
Southlake, TX 76092-3234
www.watercolorbooks.com

4th printing, 2001

To My Grandkids
Josh, Seth, Lindsay, Brandon,
Holland, Bryce and Kendal

TABLE OF CONTENTS

CHAPTER ONE

THE BASIS FOR A GREAT LIFE

John waited in the new subdivision's parked trailer for potential homebuyers whom he could sell on living in his company's newly built houses. He utilized his spare time to learn principles about business and marketing that would help him sell out this fashionable development.

Reading a book one night, John learned a principle about money that he'd never known. He applied its truth, and his career skyrocketed. Someone entered the trailer to buy a home, but instead hired John at a new start-up company. As John followed turns in his career path over the next few years, he stuck with his principles and ended up buying the company where he worked. Based on what he'd learned, he pushed productivity to new highs, which secured him a prosperous lifestyle and a great future for his family.

Everything in life is based on principle. John learned in a dramatic way that if he would change from living on the basis of personality to principles, it would change his life.

Principles are basic truths, fundamental laws of the universe, facts of nature, and primary units of life. The "law of gravity" is a principle of the universe. Isaac Newton discovered the principle and changed the nature of physical science, securing his place in world history.

Discovering principles is a lifelong passion for people who succeed. People who live by personality, preference or prejudice have no bedrock on which to build their lives and end up failing. Their foundation is shifting, movable, unsteady. People who make decisions by personality or preference can be talked out of their decisions from one day to the next. People who make decisions by prejudice can be dead wrong, have it proved to them, yet remain steadfast on the wrong path doing the wrong thing in the wrong way.

The more you build your life on principle, the higher your highs, the straighter your path, and the greater your life.

FINDING THE RIGHT PATTERN

All of life is based on principles and follows patterns. Patterns are ways in which the universe operates. Seedtime and harvest is a pattern. Tides clean the earth according to a pattern. Birds fly south, babies develop, stocks rise and fall, all according to patterns natural to the world in which we live.

You become successful and prosper when you base your life on principles and find the patterns that work for you.

Gladys learned a pattern for home sales that fit her personality and the amount of time she wanted to invest. She perfected the pattern, taught it to her three sons, and became one of the top twenty real estate professionals in the country. She is still tops today after many years, and she still practices the same pattern.

In his popular book *Rich Dad Poor Dad*, Robert Kiyosaki identified patterns for parenting that varied between middle and lower class fathers and upper income fathers. His book sold well because he taught a pattern people could understand and follow. The book, *The Millionaire Next Door*, uncovered millionaires' patterns and made them available to everyone. Discovering and uncovering workable patterns is one of the aims of successful management, corporations, and individuals.

The pattern you learn determines the life you live. The better the pattern, the better the life.

BOOKS ARE YOUR BEST FRIEND

What you have in your hands right now is your most valuable commodity today, because it contains patterns and principles to enable you to prosper in the totality of your life—in your finances, family, career and community. Recognize the patterns, learn the principles, and prosper.

An old adage says a dog is man's best friend. It's wrong. Books are people's best friends. At times books are even better than people, because books speak without an accent, using our own voice. The practice of reading books develops the power of concentration and creative thinking. It provides greater understanding, sharpness of mind, and enjoyment of life.

To learn life's most valuable patterns and principles, read what others have already uncovered before you. No scientist today still tries to discover the basic law of gravity. How gravity works is already written in books. Patterns and principles that will make you rich are readily available for you if you'll read.

Reading is an art form, enabling every reader to be an artist. Television, CD-ROM, and audiocassettes are great technological advances, but they do not compare to the skill of reading. In the last thousand years, the Gutenberg Press is still the greatest invention on earth because it allowed people to read for themselves. The common person stops the habit of reading after his schooling, but the uncommon person continues to read and study all through life. Reading makes you uncommon. And unusual. And, reading is an agent against aging. *The loss of the habit of reading is a gain in the realm of ignorance.*

A love for reading can and should be transmitted generation to generation. Listening is the first thing you learn in life, speaking is next, reading is third and writing is fourth. Today, parents teach the first two, then turn their children over to professionals, but it wasn't always so. In 1644, Massachusetts passed a law making fathers responsible for teaching children to read. It was a good law. *Reading is the most inexpensive thing a parent can do with a family—not reading is the most expensive.*

Parents misrepresent their role to their children when they leave the child's discipline and education to the other spouse or to the schools. Reading is the ingredient in child development that bonds parent and child closer and easier than any other.

Too often, parents try to solve their children's problems rather than reading to them and letting truth do its own wonderful work. Parents wait until a crisis or particular need occurs, then try to lay the solution on the child. If they had simply read sound principles day by day to their children, the work would have been done, and the answers already learned.

Our culture today advocates the visual—watching entertainment and videos. Culture is the culprit in the rise of ignorance. The book in your hand is a weapon against the cultural malaise of our day.

Only truth can set people free. Books have an infinite life expectancy because the truths they contain can never die. Truth never wears out. Truth is timeless. But truth is like soap. It's only good when it's applied. Act on what you learn. One principle can change your life, marriage or career beginning today. For that reason, I don't spoon-feed, coddle or water down the truths, but give you patterns and principles straight, like a drink from a fire hose.

Once a book is written, its life is in the reader's hands. Books are not a matter of dollars and cents, time or no time. They are a matter of life and death.

THE PATTERN OF LEVELS

Business is not about money or toys, but the level of life on which you want to live. The better your business, the higher the level of life you'll achieve. This is a pattern. *Life is lived on levels that are arrived at in stages*. At each stage you choose to move forward or fall back.

Thomas worked hard in an entry-level position at his company's customer service telephone center. His friend Jeremy always ribbed him during lunch for being the best in his group, serving more customers per day than anyone. Thomas took the friendly ribbing, appreciating being admired. The manager over Thomas' supervisor noticed his terrific call record and made an appointment to offer Thomas a promotion.

The company had a more advanced call center where operators handled high-volume customers. Thomas at first learned quickly. But by his second week in the new call center, Thomas was morose. He missed having lunch with his friends and he was embarrassed at being the worst in his division, instead of the best. As his attitude soured, his learning curve dropped and soon he was back in the manager's office because his new supervisor complained.

"Don't you like the call center?" the manager asked. "You know the pay is better."

"Nah," Thomas said. "I really don't like it there. I can't explain it."

Three weeks after Thomas returned to the lower paying job in the entry-level customer service center, the manager offered his friend Jeremy the same opportunity.

"You won't like it there," Thomas said. "You're going to end up right back here like I did."

Jeremy was nervous and listened to the warning, but wanted to try anyway. Three months later, Jeremy had mastered a new set of skills and was named shift supervisor.

Both Thomas and Jeremy determined their own level of life. Thomas refused to follow a pattern that made him start at the bottom of a new level, preferring instead to fall back to a position where he could be king. People all the time are stumped by this pattern, returning in their minds to their "glory days" as prom queen or debate team president, rather than starting from the bottom of a higher level.

Passing through the stages of life that take us to new levels is a lifelong pattern that is inescapable for those who pursue success. *The only way to avoid starting at the bottom of a new level is to avoid success.*

YOUR POWER OF CHOICE

The level on which you live is under your power of choice. *Once you make a choice, you become the servant to that choice.*

For Thomas, once he chose to return to a comfortable position, he became the servant to his choice, which included lower pay and no opportunity for advancement.

Jeremy became a servant to his choice, which included the benefits of advancement and better pay with potential for even more money.

A public school administrator watched a video I'd made about the power of choice and realized it applied to his weight as well as to his career. He looked at the piece of pizza he was about to eat that night and my words darted through his mind, "*You have the freedom to choose, but once the choice is made, you become the servant of that choice.*"

He lifted that piece of pizza to his face and looked at it instead of putting it in his mouth. "Pizza, you are under my power of choice, and I refuse to be your servant," he said, then set it down and ate a piece of fruit instead.

Over the next several days he looked at each food item he wanted to eat and made a decision whether he wanted to become the servant of that food. His eating habits changed as he exercised his power of choice over every bite of food. He lost over sixty pounds.

A corollary is, *decision translates into energy.* Indecision saps energy. The man had never been able to diet successfully, but once he made a decision, his decision translated into energy that enabled him to achieve his goals.

A woman wakes up on Saturday morning and can't decide whether to go shopping with her friend or stay home and clean the house. Her indecision leaves her listless so she drinks coffee and reads the newspaper, and doesn't get anything done. Her indecision sapped her energy. *Choosing not to decide becomes a decision in itself.*

Seth didn't have time to go to school, but was barely getting by on the amount of money he was earning at his full-time job. On the day he was laid off, he made a decision to pursue his dreams, which meant he needed to find a new job and enroll in school. He surfed the Internet, pursued the company he chose and got the job. Then he explored schools in his area and enrolled to fill up his free time. He was able to complete fulltime studies and at the same time received repeated promotions at work. His decision translated into energy, an energy he never knew he had before he made the decision.

RECOGNIZE YOUR POWER

Life is composed of your choices. Circumstances do not determine your level of life. What you do with circumstances determines your level in living.

I'll never forget a man I fired years ago for his failure to perform. The next time I saw him, he was on his way to a class to learn how to apply for welfare. If he had put as much into his job as he did into filing for welfare, he would have still had a job. He had a golden opportunity to become a manager but gave in to a welfare mentality.

When Seth was laid off, he could have moped around, found the first job that would have him, and stayed there, filling his off-hours with friends who had no more ambition than that. But he made a choice that would help compose the rest of his life.

Throughout my life, I have found that each new level requires more of me than I want to give. Yet the more given, the more obtained. At each stage, I make the critical choice again either to push forward or move to a fallback position. My life has been composed by the choices I made at each new stage.

If you don't like the life you're living, then change your choices. Choices determine conduct, character and destiny.

The only insurance you have against tomorrow is the choice you make today.

Seth is my grandson, and the greatest day of his life was the day he realized that his choices controlled his destiny. Because of events in his childhood, he had adopted the belief that life just happened, and all he could do was react to what happened. He finally came to believe that he could choose what happened.

His was the mentality of much of America today—a "victim mentality" that has propelled an era of "excuse abuse." Claiming victim status excuses people from responsibility for their own choices. It also creates frivolous lawsuits that clog our judicial system. "A culture of excuse" is what the editor of *Reason* magazine called it. The answer to that is: there is no excuse. You alone are responsible for the choices you make, so make them wisely.

Choices have consequences. I learned my own lesson at Seth's age when I tried to out-drink my father. He was emotionally absent from our home, so my mother oversaw my upbringing. On the night that I could still stand even after he passed out from the whiskey we were drinking, that hollow victory led to my discovery that choices have consequences. My choice to outdo my dad was destroying my future. It was my responsibility alone to change my choices in order to change my future.

Refusing to exercise your power of choice allows others to exercise it for you. *Allowing others to make your choices for you allows them to create your world, and when they do, they always make it too small.* No one can see or fully understand what is in your own mind and heart. That's between you and God. You can chafe and complain about the constraints within which you're being forced to live, but the truth is, regardless of your circumstances, you still have choices about your life.

YOUR SECOND TOOL

Life is composed of our choices, and it is constructed by our words. Once you make the choice to build a new life, change your words.

You are only committed to what you confess. If you don't say it, you won't feel responsible or compelled to do it, and no one will have heard it to help you be accountable.

Repeating phrases to ourselves, chanting mantras, and making positive confessions have gained popularity because leaders and coaches have realized that words build relationships—even the relationship we have with ourselves and with our world. Japanese management has practiced this for years, leading their employees in morning exercises, which include shouting out the company philosophy or slogans.

Our words build our lives. Every word we speak has creative power. We release our creative power through our words and set the world around us in motion.

How did the Chrysler Building rise from the dust of the earth? Because someone used words to build their dream. How did the Empire State Building eclipse its height? Because someone said the words, "We can do better, and I'll prove it."

Our worlds are framed by our words. During the court-contested presidential election between Al Gore and George Bush, after a particularly overwhelming loss in a lower court, Al Gore's attorney David Boies said, "Now we're getting someplace where we can get a real decision." He was appealing to the State Supreme Court, but chose words that would lead the world to believe his loss made him one step closer to victory. Al Gore's supporters rallied because their world was framed by David Boies' words, and they believed Gore's win was imminent. Even after the final decision, the words that rang in their ears were Boies', and they had a difficult time following Gore in his concession to Bush.

Words have creative power. Use your words foolishly, break your word, or take your word lightly, and you will have difficulty throughout life. Use your words wisely and you will prosper. Your choices and your words are two of your best tools.

CHOOSE TO CHANGE!

The only constant in maturity is change. Change is imminent, inevitable and important. If you grow any older, build a business, start a family, or make more money—whatever you do, you're going to experience change. *It is difficult to live with change, but impossible to live without it.*

Many years ago I had a friend who died. After he died, his widow kept their house the same way, organized her day the same way, watched the same television programs in the evenings. She spent all her energy trying to keep everything exactly the same as if he were still alive. As much as I respected him, I wanted to shout at her, "He's dead!"

As uncomfortable as it may make us, life is going to change. Life goes on regardless of what we think ought to happen. Refusing to change just ensures us of staying where we are, or losing ground. In this widow's case, her efforts to remain the same were actually causing her to lose a measure of life because it was speeding by without her.

When the personal computer, facsimile machine and FedEx changed the way America did business, people who adapted to and embraced the change moved quickly into the new era, but businesses that failed to adapt and refused to change, lost ground.

Montgomery Ward was a powerhouse retailer for years, but when Wal-Mart, Target and then the Internet changed the way Americans shopped, Wards didn't change. Sears adapted and made changes. Sears outlived Montgomery Ward.

To change from one level to the next requires stepping out of a comfort zone, dying to an old vision, breaking away from a comfortable way of thinking. If we want a different life, we have to change what we're doing. To repeat a popular statement, "the definition of insanity is doing the same thing the same way, but expecting different results."

BE WILLING TO LEARN

The man who knows how will always have a job; the man who knows why will always be his boss. You can learn how to do something, but if you master the pattern by which it works, or the principle on which it rests, you will always rise above your peers. Principles are like keys to unlock doors that were formerly closed to you. Patterns are like maps to guide you from one level to the next.

Learning life's patterns and principles is a lifelong pursuit. You are never too old, and never too young to learn. It is more common than not for people to have more than one career. The business I ended up in, I started when I was well over fifty years old. My brother-in-law, Jimmy, lost his job during a recession and could not regain his position in that field. As a result, he retrained himself and launched into a new career when he was sixty years old.

Availability is not the most important thing in the world, teachability is. A person may be available, but if they are not willing to learn, they will soon be available again. To learn, all that is required is a heart for truth and a desire to be taught. The reason Jimmy and I were able to start over is that we were willing to learn, even if it meant listening to younger people!

It is hard to tell someone something they think they already know. Open yourself to new ideas. Learn to adapt to new technologies. Get "out of the box" and realize there may be more to what you think you know. Stubbornness is the core of ignorance, because an ignorant person is too stubborn to learn. Shun ignorance! Read. Learn the principles. Master the patterns. Have the courage to change.

- Everything in life follows a pattern, based on a principle.

- The more you build your life on principle, the higher your highs, the straighter your path, and the greater your life.

- The pattern you learn determines the life you live. The better the pattern, the better the life.

- Books are people's best friends.

- Reading is an art form, enabling every reader to be an artist.

- Reading is an agent against aging.

- The loss of the habit of reading is a gain in the realm of ignorance.

- Reading is the most inexpensive thing a parent can do with a family—not reading is the most expensive.

- Culture is the culprit in the rise of ignorance.

- Truth is like soap. It's only good when it's applied.

- Life is lived on levels that are arrived at in stages.

- Once you make a choice, you become the servant to that choice.

- Decision translates into energy. Indecision saps energy.

- Choosing not to decide becomes a decision in itself.

- Life is composed of your choices and constructed by your words.

- Circumstances do not determine your level of life. What you do with circumstances determines your level of life.

- Each new level requires more. The more given, the more obtained.

- If you don't like the life you're living, then change your choices.

- Choices determine conduct, character and destiny.

- The only insurance you have against tomorrow is the choice you make today.

- There is no excuse. You alone are responsible for the choices you make.

- Choices have consequences.

- Allowing others to make your choices for you allows them to create your world, and when they do, they always make it too small.

- You are only committed to what you confess.

- Words have creative power.

- Our worlds are framed by our words.

- The only constant in maturity is change.

- It is difficult to live with change, but impossible to live without it.

- The man who knows how will always have a job; the man who knows why will always be his boss.

- You are never too old and never too young to learn.

- Availability is not the most important thing in the world, teachability is.

- It is hard to tell someone something they think they already know.

- Stubbornness is the core of ignorance.

CHAPTER TWO

DREAM YOUR FUTURE, THEN DO IT

The most powerful thing you can do in life is to create an image. Everyone from National Football League owners to Madison Avenue knows that "Image is everything." From the logo on Tiger Woods' hat to the picture of the student in Tiananmen Square, images compel and propel us.

The images in our minds drive us toward our destiny. Dreams are the substance of every great achievement in life. Bill Gates dreamed of being bigger than IBM, which was unthinkable, but he did it.

People's dreams of achievement are the basis for what they do—or don't do—in life. Muggsy Bogues dreamed of playing professional basketball. When he barely grew past five feet, he refused to let go of his dream, and he achieved it.

Clarence Thomas dreamed of becoming a lawyer. Abandoned by his parents, unable to articulate clearly, his ghetto upbringing didn't bode well for his success. But he never gave up his dream and today he sits on the United States Supreme Court.

Fred Smith is part of modern American folklore because he turned in a college project and received a low grade on it. The dream he described in his term paper, Federal Express, the university professor considered "unrealistic." But Fred didn't let go of his dream, and he achieved it.

Most people don't dream big enough. They give others the power to destroy the image in their own minds, and fail to achieve what they could have achieved. *The most powerful thing you can do in life is create an image. The next most powerful is to destroy an image.*

Go to any bar in town and you'll meet the woulda-coulda-shoulda crowds of Bills and Muggs and Clarences and Freds who allowed others to steal their dreams. When their dreams died, a new dream arose for a mundane, mediocre life, and they accepted it. Dreams can die, vanish, or be stolen, but no person can live without a dream.

SEEING YOUR FUTURE

"Dreams are the substance of achievement" is a principle of life. The image in your mind determines your future. Your dreams draw you toward your future like a magnet. The more specific your dream, the more powerful the pull. A dream that has been stolen and replaced with something like, *"You'll turn out just like your dad,"* will change your future because you'll be drawn to the negative instead of the positive.

If your dream has been altered, destroyed or transformed into a negative, you must recreate your dream into a positive vision of your future. A positive vision creates hope, a sense of destiny, and purpose.

Doug was raised in a stepfamily and barely knew his father. Although he was a champion high school wrestler whose coach wanted him to try out for the Olympics, Doug opted for drugs instead and ended up riding boxcars across the country in search of his biological father. His dream for success as an athlete dimmed because of the deeper dream in his heart to meet his father.

The meeting was less than successful, but accomplished a purpose because it allowed Doug to dream again. Sitting in the office of an exercise studio he eventually managed, he dreamed of helping lost young people and addicts get off the streets. Within a few years, Doug's dream grew to organizing all the relief organizations of his city, a dream that seemed completely out of reach since they were all competing for the same dollars to stay open. But Doug realized that dream and is now taking his plan nationally and internationally to help others. Doug's dreams drove him to his destiny. First to a negative, then, with a new dream, to a positive.

In a meeting with my friend A. R. Bernard of Brooklyn, New York, he taught that because our vision is our future, *a person without a vision is a person without a future, and a person without a future will always return to his past.* Without a vision for the future, the only vision we have is our past. That's all we can see. So if our vision is threatened, we start looking back to what we can see. And if our vision dies, we'll head back there, thinking we were better off before trying to achieve our dream.

The used car salesman who launches out in business for himself and sees it falter—where does he go? Back to the used car lot. He loses his future, so all he knows to do is what he's done before. Probation officers always find out everything about a criminal's past, so they'll know where to find him if he runs.

True in business. True in crime. True in marriage.

When there's a problem in marriage, and either spouse loses their vision for that marriage, they immediately think of returning to single life, or even to a former lover.

Just as a seed falls into the ground and dies to produce a plant many times larger than the seed, so also our vision can fall into the ground and seem to die. When a vision dies, we can have faith for its resurrection, or adopt another vision. But we can't live without a vision.

WRITE THE VISION

A dream doesn't become a goal until you write it down. Remember, you are only committed to what you confess. Write the vision you have for your future, confess it and commit it to paper, and it will become achievable.

Dreams without goals are like cars without gas. They go nowhere. Fred Smith may have received a poor grade on his project called "Federal Express," but by writing it down, he was well on his way toward achieving his dream.

Then you must believe what you've written. Seeing it in writing makes it seem real.

Glenn and Bobby were teenaged brothers who created a synthetic belt in their garage that they thought would help people lose weight. They had a vision, wrote down their plan, and saw it in practical terms. Then they created a box in which to package it and sold a few from their home. But they believed they could do something larger than a home-based business.

Putting together what money they had, they flew to K-Mart headquarters and showed their one product to the buyers. K-Mart bought it. Overnight, they were in business with production, administration and marketing to handle. Soon inventors came to them to show their products and Glenn and Bobby ended up with a fitness company that does business today worldwide.

Dreaming without doing is folly. Doing what you dream is wise. But you have to believe your dream. What you believe has the greatest potential for good or harm in your life because you are harnessed to your beliefs. Right believing has a light burden, wrong believing has a heavy burden.

All wrong conduct is based on wrong believing. I had a business friend who believed he could have an affair with his secretary without consequence. He lost his job and his family. Another friend thought he could alter documents that he sent through the mail. He served a prison sentence. Adulterers believe no one will find out. Embezzlers believe they can cover it up. Addicts believe they can handle it. Criminals believe it is somebody else's fault.

To change your conduct, change your beliefs. If you believe you're going to be poor, you'll overspend. If you believe you're dumb, you'll under-study. If you believe you're going to be killed, you'll avoid going out. If you believe people won't like you, you'll stop meeting people. But if you believe you're going to be thin, you'll eat right. If you believe you're going to succeed, you'll look for opportunities. If you believe you're going to be rich, you'll invest. If you believe you can achieve your dreams, you'll pursue them.

Perceptions create personal realities. What we believe, whether true or false, is real to us. The more our perceptions align with truth, the more prosperous we can become because truth sets us free.

ATTRACT OR REPEL

You can be one of the world's thousands of disappointments, or one of its few successes. What you think in your heart determines what you become. Believe you're a success, you'll act successful while digging ditches. Believe you're a failure, you'll act like a failure in a penthouse office.

What you believe will either attract or repel. A penthouse can't fight your own belief that you're a failure, and you'll end up digging ditches. Believe you're a success, the ditch won't be able to hold you and you'll end up in the penthouse.

You are yoked to your beliefs. *The yoke you wear determines the burden you bear*. The weight of believing *"I cannot"* is the burden of failure. The ease of believing *"I can"* is the burden of success. Positive believing is light on the mind and body, and makes the difference between minimum wage and high income.

Faith and fear have the same definition. Faith is believing what you cannot see will come to pass. Fear is believing what you cannot see will come to pass. *Faith attracts the positive, while fear attracts the negative*. The sum total of our lives is based on whether we operate on fear or faith.

A train exploded in a tunnel sending out plumes of smoke that asphyxiated panicking passengers. Most of the passengers operated from the fear that they were going to die and ran without thinking uphill into clouds of smoke and to their death. Some of the passengers operated on the faith that they would survive and stopped to think of which way to run, then ran downhill, away from the smoke to safety.

Faith attracts light, life and love. Fear attracts darkness, death and downfalls. My daughter has a happy little border collie that loves to visit my house. We have two cats at my house, Jasmine and Bandit. Jasmine is afraid of the dog and runs from it, which the dog sees as an invitation for the chase. Bandit is an older cat and unafraid of the dog. He lounges on the floor with faith that the dog will ignore him, and the dog does. *Fear attracts attack*.

In finances, when we put faith to work, faith attracts increase. People with faith launch out before waiting for perfect conditions which never come. People with faith buy low when no one else is buying and sell high when everyone else sees the

28

results of their faith. People with faith work with the little they have rather than waiting for the abundance they need.

Every person has a measure of faith. When we put faith to work, it only takes as much as the size of a mustard seed to see our dreams come true.

Faith is like the wind—it cannot be seen, only its evidence. The evidence that we are using faith is in our works. *Faith is belief in action.*

YOUR BEST FRIENDS

As you read this—whether at home with your family, on an airplane, in your office, at the beach—you are sitting with your best friend and worst enemy. It is not the person on your right or left, not an angel or devil on your shoulders. It is you. Your choices, based on what you believe, will make you your own best friend or worst enemy.

Water always seeks its own level. In terms of human life, this means you will always rise to the level of your faith. If you believe you can make thousands per month, and move into a business that produces only hundreds, you will find a way to grow that business into thousands. If you have faith for hundreds per month and move into a business that produces thousands thinking you've hit the jackpot, the business will soon level out at hundreds per month.

The hidden dream of your heart and the exercising of your faith will result in the way you live and the level you achieve. Not everyone lives on the same level of faith. Not all share the same vision. To guard your vision, you must guard what you allow into your life.

As you rise from one level of life to another, your intimate friendships must change. Retaining close associations with those who refuse to grow will frustrate your own growth. Your closest friends, when they don't share your vision, can become your chief critics and worst dream-killers.

PRIVATE BELIEFS BECOME PUBLIC KNOWLEDGE

Guard your beliefs.

If you accept someone else's philosophy that is merely a rationalization to justify their failure, you accept their failure. When you live by someone's failed philosophy, you live their failure.

A missionary came home from overseas after leading a church of 100 people. He was placed in charge of a denomination's foreign missions department, and developed what he called the "mother church" concept. In it, he recommended that churches only grow to 100, then spin off new members to start another church. The missionary adopted the philosophy to justify his failure of never having over a hundred in church. Anyone who accepts his philosophy accepts his failure. Anyone knows there is strength in numbers.

Guard your beliefs. The combination of all your beliefs creates your private philosophy. *Private philosophy determines public performance.*

A lie has spread in our society that what a person does in private is his own business. The lie was started to justify the immoral activities of political, religious and business leaders to make their failings amenable to the public. But it became a philosophy so pervasive that people believed it not just about leaders, but about themselves, thinking they could live any way they wanted and it shouldn't affect their work or family or public life.

When a lie is created to justify someone's moral failure, those who accept it accept the failure.

No man is an island. None of us lives or dies to ourself. What we do in private affects ourselves, our families, and society when it becomes public. "Be sure your sins will find you out," is more than a cliché repeated by schoolmarms. Whatever is done in secret will one day be shouted from the housetops.

In politics, what a person practices in private determines how he or she will vote in public. In the movie industry, because of the private philosophy of a handful of decision-makers, America has sent videos worldwide that have debilitated traditional customs, and devalued national morals. In the stock market, the private belief of entrepreneurs that it was more important to secure funding than to sell a viable product, sent stocks plunging and created financial ruin for many.

What is practiced in private is eventually seen in public. And the person you really are is best seen by what you do when you are all alone.

Guard your beliefs. *The only principle you really believe is the one you obey.*

GOOD, BETTER, BEST

Good is the enemy of best. The best comes not with perfection but simply when you can do no better. If you know you can do better, then you haven't done your best. That belief is what drives a Phil Jackson with a basketball team and a Venus Williams on the tennis court. It's what motivates Martha Stewart with each new enterprise and Cecilia Bartoli with each new opera.

Why settle for good when you can have the best? As I look back over the years, most people I have known could have had more if they hadn't settled for less.

Go for greatness. Every good thing in life begins with you, so make it happen. Write your vision, then act in faith on your beliefs, according to your personal philosophy.

- The most powerful thing you can do in life is to create an image. The next most powerful is to destroy an image.

- Dreams are the substance of every great achievement in life.

- Your vision determines your future.

- A person without a vision is a person without a future, and a person without a future will always return to his past.

- Dreams without goals are like cars without gas. They go nowhere.

- Dreaming without doing is folly. Doing what you dream is wise.

- What you believe has the greatest potential for good or harm in your life.

- Right believing has a light burden, wrong believing has a heavy burden.

- All wrong conduct is based on wrong believing.

- To change your conduct, change your beliefs.

- You can be one of the world's thousands of disappointments, or one of its few successes.

- What you believe will either attract or repel.

- You are yoked to your beliefs. The yoke you wear determines the burden you bear.

- Faith is believing what you cannot see will come to pass. Fear is believing what you cannot see will come to pass.

- Faith attracts the positive. Fear attracts the negative.

- Faith is like the wind—it cannot be seen, only its evidence.

- Faith is belief in action.

- You are sitting with your best friend and worst enemy. You.

- Water always seeks its own level.

- As you rise from one level of life to another, your intimate friendships must change.

- If you accept someone else's philosophy that is merely a rationalization to justify their failure, you accept their failure. When you live by someone's failed philosophy, you live their failure.

- Private philosophy determines public performance.

- The only principle you really believe is the one you obey.

- Good is the enemy of best.

- If you know you can do better, then you haven't done your best.

- You could have more if you don't settle for less.

- Every good thing in life begins with you, so make it happen.

CHAPTER THREE

SEEK TRUE WEALTH

Wealth and riches are not synonymous. Wealth will get you riches, but riches will never make you wealthy.

True wealth comes from your character. Succeeding in business at the expense of your family will leave you no more fulfilled than living in poverty. Gifts, talents, knowledge and wisdom help give you the power to get wealth, but wealth is only realized when these are coupled with a degree of spiritual, mental, emotional and physical health.

Jim produced riches and a comfortable lifestyle when he ran a development company with fifty employees. But he moved from riches to wealth when he fired everyone, bought two cellular telephones, and started working with sub-contractors out of his house. Fewer people and projects, less physical exertion, coupled with his natural talent and wisdom, produced for him peace of mind and a truly wealthy life that brought him riches.

Buddy produced riches when he started his own publishing company and helped fledgling authors. But he produced wealth when he added more publishing companies, built other businesses and was able to fulfill his heart's desire to help more people than a mere handful of authors.

Viland thought he'd made a success in management for an international corporation. He wore nice clothes, drove terrific cars and paid for his daughter's private education. One morning he woke up and did not want to go to work.

A few weeks later, he realized he always hated going to work. Worse, he didn't care for the things his work enabled him to buy.

Viland's wife, Kathy, was worried when he told her he needed a change, but she went along with him as he resigned, sold their cars and bought a pickup truck. Then he bought an old fixer-upper in a middle-class neighborhood and set to work with his hands. The house sold, he made a good profit, and he bought two more.

Today Viland has two crews working for him. He wears stained Levis as he buys his coffee at the doughnut shop with the other contractors each morning, then drives the pickup to his job sites and planning meetings, pitching in where needed to receive the satisfaction he gets from working with his hands. He bought his wife a nice car again, his daughter never felt the transition, and his earnings have leveled off where they were with the company. Before he had riches. Now he has wealth.

FIND YOUR GIFTS

It is common knowledge that cheating in business produces a curse, not the blessing people were seeking when they cheated. In the same way, producing riches by doing what you hate is a form of cheating yourself. It will not result in the prosperity you seek. Money cannot compensate for lack of personal fulfillment.

God created each of us uniquely, but not equally. I'll let you take me shopping or golfing to prove that to you. I'm not the best at either. We each have the capacity for excellence, but not by exercising the same gifts as everyone else. One look at the fish of the sea, and you can see the earth thrives on diversity. *You are not like anyone else on earth, and you're not supposed to be.*

You can be in the same line of work as someone else, and succeed at it, but you'll do it in a different way. No two people will do any job exactly alike. A good artist can paint a bowl of fruit, but two artists painting the same bowl of fruit will end up with two entirely different paintings. One is not bad and the other good. They're just different. They're supposed to be.

One motivational expert liked the way another motivational speaker conducted her seminars. He changed his entire organization and even his own manner of speaking in order to do what had made the woman so successful. He failed. Rather than putting the principles to work that had made the woman's seminars work, or adopting her pattern to his own strengths and abilities, he tried to copy exactly what she did. It was a disaster from which he has still not entirely recovered.

Wearing another person's pattern for life is like trying to run a race in shoes that don't fit. You can follow the principles and the pattern, but you must accentuate your *own* gifts and excel in your *own* strengths. Revel in what you do well! Celebrate your talents!

The greatest realization of personal prosperity will come when you discover and exercise your God-given gifts and achieve a goal for which you can say, "I was born for this." Gifts and talents are never earned, only discovered. Your greatest fulfillment will be found in the place where you utilize your gifts and talents.

YOU NEED OTHER PEOPLE'S HELP

Most people are more aware of what they do wrong than what they do right. What happened when you brought home your report card as a child? There were perhaps congratulations for the high marks, but you were left with a demand to pull up the low marks. It's usually the negative that sticks with us. And it often sticks for life.

Weaknesses need not have power over strengths and strengths need not be tainted by weaknesses. They are entirely different issues. My friend John Binkley pointed out that if you spend all your time on your weaknesses, the most you can hope to become is average. But if you focus energy on your strengths, there is no limit to what you can produce. Uncover your strengths. Then go to them.

Other people can see your strengths before you do, because to you they seem common. Ask your friends. Lynn networks well, presents herself in a positive manner and has never met a stranger. Ask her about her strengths, though, and she looks lost for a moment before she can answer. The greatest strength she possesses comes to her so naturally, she forgets it's a gift. If it seems like anyone could do it, that's likely one of your strengths.

Ask yourself what stirs your creative juices. Pay attention to what fills your waking thoughts, what you feel drawn toward during recreation and relaxation. Those are clues to find your strengths. When you find your strengths, you find your pathway to total life prosperity.

All of life depends on relationships. You need people not just to show you your strengths, but to cover your weaknesses. An old axiom says it's not what you know but who you know. The perversion of the principles implies you are to use people for personal profit, then discard them. But the principle is true. Find someone with strengths in the areas of your weaknesses. Partner with people who are strong where you are weak, so you can go to your strengths while they cover your weaknesses.

When I want tickets to a basketball game, I call a professional player who is a friend. He leaves the tickets for me at Will Call. Big deal for me. No big deal for him. Why? Because he has a means to get tickets and I don't. When he needs advice or help in his various enterprises, he calls me. I listen to him on the telephone, tell him what I think and hang up. Big deal for him. No big deal for me. Why? Because I know the principles he doesn't know.

It's not *what* you know, but *who* you know. Call it a barter system or a partnership, it's just good business. Find people who are strong in areas where you're weak and you'll be able to go to your strengths. *Focus on your strengths and your weaknesses become irrelevant.*

People earning annually a quarter million dollars or more listed five primary factors in achieving success:

Communication skills
Intelligence – not just education, but common sense
Integrity
Experience
A positive attitude

I pass these along because they are not just a basis for acquiring wealth, but a basis for acquiring relationships that will help you.

Pitfalls to Achieving Wealth

Three things sabotage success: The lust of the flesh, the lust of the eyes and the pride of life. Every temptation for evil in human life emanates from, is originated by, or is initiated from, those three.

Look at pride. "Pride goes before a fall," the proverb states. Humility is the opposite of pride. Humility precedes blessing. If you have trouble with pride, don't try to squash it, just start practicing humility and pride will take care of itself. True humility is not denying how great you are, talking bad about yourself, deprecating your gifts, or denying your abilities. *True humility is simply the willingness to remain anonymous.* "There is no limit to the good a man can do if he doesn't care who gets the credit," states the old adage.

You can practice humility today in any number of ways. Allow someone to go first at the stop sign. Signal a pedestrian to walk in front of you. Give an extra-large tip to your server. Then keep your good deeds to yourself. Those are simple exercises, but they will produce a change of attitude from within. The next time you want to brag about your income or demand of a clerk, *"Do you know who I am?,"* you'll have a string of successes behind you that enable you to stay humble.

Anonymity is the essence of true humility. "Overnight successes" always come from those who have spent a lifetime on work that nobody saw. I am always amazed in sports to see that it's just a hundredth of a second, a tenth of a point, a tiny movement, that sets apart the winners from the losers. Working all alone, burgeoning athletes start humble because they don't know if they'll make the team, earn the title or win the gold. But after they achieve success, I am equally amazed at how few remain humble. In their pride, they spend their fortunes, ruin their public relations, and often end their lives in poverty of spirit as well as money.

Heisman trophies and championship rings are not uncommon in pawnshops and private collections.

It takes humility to admit what you don't know. It takes humility to admit need. It takes humility to try again. It takes humility to change. Humbling yourself to learn, keep trying and change keeps you limber, mobile, ready to advance to the next level.

Passion is the folly of youth and prejudice is the folly of old age. (I've heard prejudice called the "hardening of the attitudes.") But pride is the folly of middle age. To move successfully into what the author of *Passages* calls "second adulthood," we need the humility to admit what we have not yet learned.

Overcoming pride opens the door for you to start over on the next level. There is always a next level—and a next, and a next. A higher level exists even than fame and fortune. It is called "Greatness." Above greatness comes "Legend." Of true legends, almost all achieved their spot in history in part through their humility.

LUST AND PROSPERITY

Of the three things that sabotage success—the lust of the flesh, the lust of the eyes and pride, two-thirds stem from lust.

Lust is just perverted love. The opposite of love emotionally is hate. The opposite of love legally is law. The opposite of love morally is lust.

Love is the desire to benefit others even at the expense of self, because love desires to give. Lust desires to benefit self even at the expense of others because lust desires to get.

Anyone can lust. Nations can lust. Corporations can lust. What else would you call it when corporations sacrifice

41

their workers and relationships in order to acquire another business? Or when they make a windfall and refuse to share it with their staff or consumers? It might produce a short-term profit, but it will bring destruction in the end.

A women's product at the top of its market decided to reduce the contents of its packaging while keeping the price the same. No higher costs required the cut in their services. No shortage existed. Their desire for personal gain at the expense of their customers resulted in being knocked out of first place, never to recover.

I've seen certain poor African nations with an inordinate affection for America's prosperity. When America gave in answer to their request, the upper echelon of government received the largesse, but the citizens saw no difference. The request for the gift was predicated by greed. The same country will ask again and again, and never recover from spiraling poverty because of their greed.

Yet, nations like Uganda have changed completely since I first started going there almost twenty years ago. They got rid of the lust from the old dictatorial regimes, started taking care of their citizens by working with what they had, and the country, its industries, and its private citizens are beginning to prosper as a result.

LOVE YOUR WAY TO PROSPERITY

Love is easily satisfied. Lust is insatiable. When lusts are stirred, no object is outside our reach. We lust the Lexus on the highway, the hamburger on the road sign, the woman in the Jeep Cherokee, the diamond on the other woman's finger, the food the other guy ordered, the channels our television doesn't get. *Lust has no limits and can find no ends.*

Love is the nature of heaven, and produces heaven on this earth. Lust is the nature of hell. To live a life based on lust is to produce a hell of a life.

Old television series such as "Father Knows Best" showed us love. Sure, they showed it in terms of the ideal, but it gave us something to live up to. Today, most images in our society, from billboards to song lyrics, are based on lust and give us something to live down to.

One characteristic that defines a culture is language. Culture determines civilization. The deterioration of the language of a culture is a sign of that civilization's degeneration. Regeneration is the process of love. Degeneration is the process of lust. When lust becomes the common level of language in society, rather than love and concern for others, it reveals impending danger.

Lust is seen throughout corporate America on every level. To exhibit lust is to work only for yourself. Employees who lust their jobs use every sick day, take home office supplies, use the copier for personal purposes, come in late, leave early, and spend a good deal of the day on the telephone or Internet taking care of personal business. It works both ways. Lustful managers deride employees and shift blame to make themselves look better.

To exhibit love is to work for someone else's highest good. Successful managers know that if they work toward every employee's highest productivity, the entire company will benefit. Successful employees know that if they work for their manager's highest good, they will be promoted along with the manager, or even eclipse her. The proof of love or lust in the workplace can be seen in the bottom line.

One of the signs of Mark Cuban's true prosperity is that when he sold Broadcast.com to Yahoo for $3.7 billion, 300 out of 330 employees became millionaires. He built the business based on a concern for others, not just himself. He looked out for their highest good. In return, they looked after his highest good and everyone succeeded.

Mark discovered that not all millionaires loved caviar and champagne, but they all loved free Cokes, so he stocked his company refrigerators with Cokes, which cost little, yet conveyed his care and concern for others. When he bought the faltering Dallas Mavericks basketball franchise, he applied the same pattern. He upgraded his players' beds in hotel rooms on the road. He hired someone to wash and service the cars they drove to the airport when they boarded the team plane. He spent a minute fraction of what he'd paid for the team, but it made them happy, and in one season they became winners.

Love is exhibited by working for someone's highest good.

You can love or lust yourself even. When you operate in love for your body, you take care of your health, eat right and maintain an exercise regime of some kind. Because love is easily satisfied, this lifestyle easily satisfies your appetite, and makes your body feel wholesome and well balanced. But lusting causes a craving for insatiable sweets, fats or drugs, or for keeping hours that tear down your body, yet in your lust you demand that your body still function to please you. Lust is insatiable. Your body will bear the brunt of its force.

Temptation can sabotage all you do and bring a sudden end to your quest for prosperity. Tempting thoughts tell you to seek riches, thinking they alone will bring happiness. But lust is never satisfied. Allowed to run unbridled, it will consume everything you earn as it drives you to more, bigger, faster, sooner, better. A lust for money will never produce true wealth.

STAY ON GUARD

Learn your strengths by asking others, and by listening to yourself, then find a way to go to your strengths. Find people whose strengths are in areas of your weakness and utilize skill to build relationships with them. On the pathway to prosperity, guard yourself, avoid the three basic temptations and control your passions. The principle is, "*Master your passion or your passion will master you.*"

- Wealth will get you riches, but riches will never make you wealthy.

- Money cannot compensate for lack of personal fulfillment.

- God created each of us uniquely, but not equally.

- Gifts and talents are never earned, only discovered.

- If you spend all your time on your weaknesses, the most you can hope to become is average.

- When you find your strengths, you find your pathway to total life prosperity.

- It's not what you know but who you know.

- When you focus on your strengths, your weaknesses become irrelevant.

- Every temptation for evil in human life emanates from, is originated by, or is initiated from, the lust of the flesh, the lust of the eyes or the pride of life.

- Humility precedes blessing.

- True humility is simply the willingness to remain anonymous.

- There is no limit to the good a man can do if he doesn't care who gets the credit.

- Anonymity is the essence of true humility.

- It takes humility to admit what you don't know, to admit need, to try again, to change.

- Passion is the folly of youth, pride is the folly of middle age, and prejudice is the folly of old age.

- Lust is perverted love.

- Love is the desire to benefit others even at the expense of self, because love desires to give. Lust desires to benefit self even at the expense of others because lust desires to get.

- Love is easily satisfied. Lust is insatiable.

- Love is the nature of heaven, and produces heaven on this earth. Lust is the nature of hell.

- Love is exhibited by working for someone's highest good.

- Master your passion or your passion will master you.

CHAPTER FOUR

CHARACTER COUNTS

It is always easier to obtain than to maintain. Obtaining a position on a baseball team is easier than maintaining it. Ask any player. Obtaining access to the boardroom of a publicly-held company is easier than maintaining it. Ask any top executive. Obtaining riches is easier than maintaining a strong cash flow. Ask anyone who has ever been sued or the Hunt brothers or the founder of a dotcom.

Many reasons exist for the difficulty in maintaining, but I'll give you one because it is an important principle: *It is possible for your talent to take you to a place where your character cannot sustain you.*

Two talented athletes became stars at the same time. Both fell into eclipse. One returned to working out, rebuilt his character from the inside out, and once again regained the playing field, eventually taking his team to the Super Bowl. The other depended solely on his talent and, without trying to rebuild his character, still suffers the anguish of shame for his inability to get back on the playing field. Good, strong character supports talents and abilities.

Character is always more important than talent. People can commit to character. They cannot commit to talent. I'll illustrate by giving you a choice between hiring two employees. The first employee is talented, breezes through her work and gets the job done, but is often absent, comes in late, gossips with the other staff and creates tension in the office. The other employee comes every day on time, works hard, is easy to get along with, and even though she doesn't have a great deal of flare, she always has her work done on time. Whom do you want to hire? The first is what today's business climate might accept as a "consultant," but the second is the trustworthy employee.

The Nature of Character

Character is an internal quality that is fed by external sources. Character has no self-creative powers, nor any self-corrective power. The best character is in constant need of checks and balances from without. It requires stimulus from without, so it won't fail in development. Character deteriorates over time unless it is fed from external sources. The purity of the external sources that character feeds on determines its strength.

Jamal was given the opportunity to administrate a burgeoning company, yet felt incapable of keeping up with the challenges of growth. He was determined to advance as far as possible and earn as much as possible, so he applied himself to improvement. The place he went was the library and the biographies of people he most admired. He read voraciously, making notes about the principles they lived by and the patterns they followed. After reading about those whom he knew, he read about those whom he'd never heard of, and he amassed reams of notepaper filled with words to live by. His company never exceeded his character and, after twenty years, he is the top man today.

The books you read and the people you meet are externals that help build or destroy your character. That's why you can tell the character of a person by the company he or she keeps. *Evil companionships corrupt good character.*

Quality is always determined internally, never externally. The cheaper the internal quality of merchandise, the higher the gloss needed externally. Cheap office furniture is covered with finishes, paint and shellac. But in the executive's chambers with its high quality furniture, the wood is buffed to show off its internal luster.

Cheap knives have painted plastic handles and covered pot metal blades to try to make them look right. A high quality knife has a plain bone handle with a stainless steel blade, both of which only need polish for their internal beauty to be seen. Real quality in material or character needs nothing to cover it up. What you see is what you get.

The principle is: *the cheaper the merchandise, the higher the gloss.* It's true of furniture and knives, and it's true of men and women. Good character requires no faking, no façade, no flamboyance or flare. Externals reveal what is internal, and the internal shines through.

TRUTH IS KING IN CHARACTER

Only one moral, ethical, and true foundation exists for good character: truth. Truth is the unassailable and indestructible basis for your character. The way to build good character is to base it, as Jamal did, upon your beliefs about humanity, God, duty and truth.

Opinions will not hold up to truth. Truth must be sought after, studied out, learned and rehearsed to develop good character. Truth is the rock upon which we build good character. Without good character, all accomplishments are short-lived.

Art had a mobile medical business. It was a novel idea when he started and had tremendous potential for growth. In the first year, he and his partner eclipsed every goal and projection they'd made, and the future seemed bright. But the partner became greedy. Instead of dealing with him in truth, Art tried to get from the business whatever money he could without the partner knowing. They ended up in court and the lawyers got the money. The lawyers, that is, plus the competitors who simply copied the idea, took it nation-wide and made a huge success.

Trust is extended to the limit of truth and no more. You cannot trust a partner who is dishonest. Not in business, marriage, or in public life. When our national leaders or the media do not tell or show the truth, how can they be trusted? To trust in a half truth is to trust in a whole lie. "Factoids," distorted and perverted truths, either in print, celluloid, or digital, are still untruths. They are mere personal perspectives given at the expense of truth.

We must learn truth, meditate on it, hold it as a valued and cherished treasure, to develop and maintain strong character, which translates into societal order and peaceful corporate living.

LIES MURDER TRUTH

Lies, and all that is morally wrong, inconsistent with good character, and destructive to morals and society, can never be right. Yet lies permeate society today.

"It seems lawyers have a license to lie," a lawyer once said to me. Public relations firms churn out "spin" for political elections and beleaguered corporations, to tell their version of "facts," which is overall a euphemism for "lying."

Survivors on reality-television programs are rewarded for outwitting each other, mostly by lying, and 56 million viewers tune in. Only one survivor keeps his word and the effect is shock. In America, we don't expect people to keep their word or tell the truth anymore. To many, lying is an art form. And what's wrong with that? Why make honesty an issue in a society where leaders mislead by quibbling about such things as the meaning of the word "is"?

Honesty is an issue because when truth collapses, morality has nothing on which to stand. The collapse of truth brings disaster socially and economically, both individually and corporately. Individual and national character is founded upon truth. *People and nations are not great by virtue of their wealth, but by the wealth of their virtue.*

Peru's government was rocked by the uncovering of bribes and lies by officials from the top all the way down to the lowliest legislator. The president resigned during the imbroglio, but few were qualified to replace him because the allegations cast such a wide net. The Philippines elected a charismatic leader devoid of character. His talent paved the way for his election, but his character could not sustain it and he was forced out in disgrace. As America did during the Watergate crisis, these nations suffered the collapse of truth in the upper echelons of government.

TRUTH STANDS THE TEST OF TIME

Truth is a good person's unassailable and indestructible basis for good character. Truth stands the test of time. My friend Hector is a classic example. He remembers his mother being evicted from every public building complex in his city when he was a child. He finally left her crowded apartment in the projects to seek out his biological father. The man was also down on his luck, but took Hector in.

One Sunday as they ate lunch together, his father said, "Hector, always be the first one on the job, and always be the last to leave, and no matter what happens, even if your job depends on it, never, ever tell a lie. If you've made a mistake, own up to it right away. Never try to lie your way out of anything."

It was a memorable experience because it was the best the father could do for his son at the time. Hector treated his dad's advice as a precious gift to cherish. While still in his teens, Hector struck out on his own. At a young age, a large firm noticed him and hired him as a project manager.

On the first day of the job, the partner said, "These five houses have to be ready in two weeks and the families moved in." Hector looked at the unfinished framing and with a trembling hand dialed the telephone. "Honey, I'm not going to see you for a few days," he told his wife.

The job looked impossible, but he figured the partner must know a way to get it done, so it was up to Hector to learn what the man had learned. He wrote out a 24-hour schedule for all his crews and subcontractors. A month later, the partner came to the site to see how he was faring.

"Whatever happened to those five houses anyhow?" he asked Hector.

"The families moved in two weeks ago, just like you ordered," Hector said. The man insisted on seeing the homes, and tried to conceal his wonder and admiration for the accomplishment.

A few days later, Hector received a call saying the partners wanted to send him several men to train as project managers. He tried to reason, saying he was still learning the job.

"Just teach them what you already know," the partner said, and hung up.

All five men became skilled project managers and soon Hector was working out of the main office. For three years, he continued to receive promotions, bonuses and raises. Every time he was called in to see a senior partner meant more money for him and his family, until one day when the senior partners became grim. Sitting in a dark restaurant over a cup of coffee, they asked him the question of a lifetime.

"We need to know, if there were something seriously wrong, not just a company problem, but something you know is linked to one of us, would you lie for us?"

The next few moments felt like hours as Hector pondered the question. These men trusted him, had been generous with him, and he trusted them, too. Why not lie for them? *"No matter what ..."* came his father's admonition.

"No, sir, as much as I respect you, I could not lie for you." In the back of Hector's mind he ran through the speech he would give to his wife in a few minutes to assure her that he'd find another job after losing this one.

Hector's heart pounded and his mind roared as his boss said, "If you had said yes, we would always have kept you employed because you're a good worker. But since you won't lie, we can make you an offer that we could never make to a liar. We'd like to bring you on as a junior partner."

Hector is still with the firm today and is prospering above his wildest dreams.

The senior partners knew their trust could be extended to the limit of Hector's truth. Commerce, industry and business in general are accomplished by trust. *The reward of the trustworthy is more trust.*

Telling the truth might be one of the hardest things you will ever do, but once you do it, it is the most exhilarating. The enlargement of heart, freedom from guilt, and absence of anxiety is well worth the price of a moment's discomfort.

No lie will ever serve anyone's purposes for achieving prosperity. What is wrong, inconsistent with good character, and destructive of morality and society cannot be made to be right, no matter what. We each have the option of adapting to the culture around us, which values the license to lie above the liberty to walk in truth. But in so doing, we would help destroy the foundation of our society.

The truth is always right, and a lie is always wrong. Truth must occupy the very core of our beings, our heart of hearts. Any untruth is immoral on personal grounds, and illegitimate for social reasons. There is nothing trustworthy, stable, or good in a person who lies. A person who chooses to believe lies, when he knows the truth in his heart, is foolish.

IT'S THE HEART!

President Clinton's campaign manager James Carville determined that one thing would win the election, and made famous the words, "It's the economy, Stupid!" When it comes to winning at life, the heart comes first. It's the heart!

Your heart can believe what your mind cannot conceive. When you dream your dreams and write your vision and go to your strengths and try to believe you are going to prosper, it's your heart that will carry or condemn you. Murder begins in the heart. Adultery begins in the heart. Prosperity begins in the heart. Wealth begins in the heart. The acid test of character is in your heart.

What you think in your heart determines what you become. Whatever you meditate, focus, and concentrate on will eventually drop from your head to your heart. Whatever gets from your mind to your heart determines the course of your life because it is from your heart that the issues of life spring. What is in your heart will bring you cursing or blessing, poverty or prosperity.

In the womb, our hearts are created first, then our minds. Our hearts have their own memories that lay deeper than our minds. If our minds are the outboard motors, our hearts are the navigation equipment. Why did Hector obey his father's instruction fifteen years later? Because his father had spoken to his heart.

Our thoughts matter. Our creed is vital. Our beliefs are basic. All feed our heart and program it to propel us toward prosperity and to believe what our minds may not be able to conceive.

Truth is the standard or basis for good character. It is the only absolute. No solid and impregnable character can be built on any other foundation than truth. You can pitch your personality, but you build your character. *And when the charm wears off, you have nothing but character left.* It's in the heart.

- It is always easier to obtain than to maintain.
- It is possible for your talent to take you to a place your character cannot sustain.
- Character is always more important than talent.
- People can commit to character. They cannot commit to talent.

- The purity of the external sources that character feeds on determines its strength.

- You can tell the character of a person by the company he or she keeps.

- Evil companionships corrupt good character.

- Quality is always determined internally, never externally.

- The cheaper the merchandise, the higher the gloss.

- Only one moral, ethical, and true foundation exists for good character: truth.

- Trust is extended to the limit of truth and no more.

- To trust in a half truth is to trust in a whole lie.

- When truth collapses, morality has nothing on which to stand.

- People and nations are not great by virtue of their wealth, but by the wealth of their virtue.

- The reward of the trustworthy is more trust.

- The truth is always right, and a lie is always wrong.

- Your heart can believe what your mind cannot conceive.

- What you think in your heart determines what you become.

- You can pitch your personality, but you build your character.

- When the charm wears off, you have nothing but character left.

- It's in the heart.

CHAPTER FIVE

THE NATURE OF MONEY

"Too many people buy things they don't need with money they don't have to impress people they don't like." I don't know who said that first, but it's so good. The use of your money reveals your values that come from your character. If you want to see where your heart is, open your checkbook. You might try to convince your spouse of your love, but your checkbook will tell the truth.

Money represents your life. You give your time, talent, education, and experience and in return you receive money. The money you receive represents your life given at work. You give your life and you get money. That means, how you spend your money shows what you do with your life. If you want your life to count, make your money count. *Master the principles that master money.*

YOUR WORK ETHIC

You can sum up the traditional American work ethic in one phrase: *If you don't work, you don't eat.* That work ethic is being threatened today by our fascination and preoccupation with gambling. Trying to get rich quick is an illusion. Most lottery winners are broke within four years. Why? Because it is easier to obtain than to maintain. Slowly amassing our fortune allows us the time to learn how to maintain that fortune. If we win it overnight with a huge contract or in a game of cards or with the roll of the dice, we haven't mastered the skills necessary to maintain our newfound riches.

After the dotcom failures by companies that sought more start-up cash instead of producing a product, experts came out with a clear message for American industry: Produce. Dotcoms failed that lived on investor money, and never had a product that made money. Profitability is the priority in business—and serving the customer properly is the number one way to making a profit.

Learn to meet a need, and money will follow. The principle is, money follows ministry. During the Great Depression, people stood in lines for hours just for the privilege of eating in soup kitchens. One industrious man realized they needed something to pass the time. He picked up chips of wood off the ground and invented a word game called Scrabble that is still a favorite today in most American households. His fortune followed his ability to see and meet a need.

In sales, you're never selling a product, but an answer to a need. Years ago at a large insurance corporation's convention, I heard an old country insurance salesman speak. A legend in the company, he gave the pattern he had followed for years. "I just let the people talk, and then when they're done, I ask them to sign the paper." People will tell you their needs. Listen, then meet them.

The Curse of Poverty

If we feed our minds and hearts, and program our characters with truth and encouraging words, our hearts and minds will start to prosper and external financial prosperity will come.

Earlier I talked about Gladys, the successful realtor. Gladys was a bookkeeper and mother of three boys who had a dream. As she meditated on inspirational books, she set her heart on "three critical E's"—Energy, Enthusiasm, and Efficiency. Gladys consciously eliminated the negative, made inspiring friendships, recited affirmations, wrote her vision and rehearsed her goals. In addition, she changed her diet, adopted an exercise regime, relaxed often and made sure she laughed.

Launching into a new career, Gladys made a conscious decision to be enthusiastic and create an infectious, enthusiastic environment. She demanded she "do it right the first time" and use her time effectively. Gladys could have taken her "three critical E's" into any business and made a success of it. Before she ever became a success in business, she had become a success in her own heart. Her heart prospered first.

Poverty springs from the heart. People who hoard money live in poverty, regardless of how much money they have. Fearing the future and thinking only of self produces a poverty spirit that no amount of money can overcome. Misers aren't waiting until they have a certain amount before they go out and live. Even if they meet their financial goals, they'll raise those goals and keep hoarding. *Loving money ensures you'll never have money enough.*

Poverty is first in heart, then in finances. True, lasting prosperity is first in heart, then in finances.

MODERN SLAVERY

Poverty is being propelled and propagated in American society by "easy credit" that has enslaved us to debt. Debt can be defined as any payment that is overdue or, more narrowly, as anything we owe, period. Borrowing is not always bad but lending is better. Borrowing by co-signing for another person is the same as borrowing ourselves. Co-signing makes us servants to another person's debt.

Some of the wealthiest people I know say that if you manage debt, everything else will take care of itself. Managing debt is a discipline. It requires controlling our appetites and emotions. Good debt management stems from mastering our passions, rather than allowing our passions to master us.

Debt has become a modern form of slavery. We are no longer free to choose, but must stay on the job, or two jobs or three, to service our debt. Debtors are placed in bondage to their debt. Debtors become servants of lenders.

Debt is a "structural evil" in our lives today. "Structural evils" are created when an entire group buys in to a particular temptation. Temptations to do wrong always promise on the surface to serve and please but only desire to enslave and dominate. When the pleasure is gone, the consequences can last for a lifetime, or an eternity.

Marxist communism was a structural evil. The allure of communism was to end control by the privileged few, to end poverty, social classes and their resulting strife. That was the allure. But the hidden aims of Marxism were to eliminate the right to private property, dissolve the family unit, and destroy religious values. In short, communism was destined to put people in bondage.

In the same way, debt is a structural evil. The allure of debt is the easy payment plan, the simplicity of having what we want now and paying for it later. It's comfortable for us, and what we buy gives us a feeling of relief and well-being. When we sign our name, we don't see the consequences of our decision, only its pleasure. As a society, we have condoned debt, passed laws about debt, and created an entire social order based on debt. Although it's legal, debt is a hard way to live. Prosperous living is debt-free living.

CONVERSION FROM A DEBTOR'S MENTALITY

Conversion is not a religious word. Conversion takes place in every area of life. You were formed in your mother's womb in water and darkness, but through the miracle of birth, you came out of the womb to live in air and light. Your life starts with a miracle of transformation, a conversion.

In the same way, people are negative by nature and have to be converted to the positive. We never have to teach a child to say, "No," or "Mine." As the child grows, her parents have to convert her from the negative to the positive. Every good salesperson knows that "no" is always the first answer, and customers have to be converted to "yes."

Debt and poverty are negative. Prosperity is positive. We don't need get-rich schemes or another motivational series, we just need to be converted.

After we're converted, we will find debt riddled throughout our lives in many strange forms. I walked into my son's house one day to watch football and there on the sofa was a couple with whom I had once parted on bad terms. After a few minutes, I realized I owed them something, so I took the husband off to a side room and looked him eye to eye.

"I owe you an apology for what I did to offend you," I said. Then I did the same with his wife. It didn't matter how they responded, although we did renew our friendship, but in that moment I was converted from a debtor's mentality to a mindset of prosperity and promise.

I told that story to a friend in Southern California who was having difficulty with his son. He had just come from a counseling appointment where his son pointed at him and blurted, "He owes me!" My friend had promised his son on two occasions to go camping, but business hindered him from following through. My friend had to pay his debt to his son in order for their relationship to prosper.

WISDOM GIVES YOU STRATEGY

We live in a culture of debt. In order to overcome debt's negative effects, we must become powerful enough to make a break from the culture around us. We need wisdom and a strategy to break free into victory. People want to win the debt battle, but it all starts with wisdom, then a strategy. It is wisdom not to incur more debt, to make sacrifices, pay cash, and celebrate each debt paid. The principles give us the wisdom—we develop the strategy.

My friends David and Barbara had a business for which they had taken a loan to purchase equipment. They also had a mortgage on their house. But since they paid cash for everything else, they didn't consider themselves to be in debt. At a conference, a speaker said he owed nothing to anyone, and that bit of wisdom enlightened Dave and Barbara that even though they were prospering in many ways, they still owed.

They immediately began to search out wisdom that would give them a strategy. As they were discussing it, a large contract came in and Barbara realized that if they cut off every outflow of money for a few months, they could use the entire profit to pay off their equipment loan. Once done, the extra cash each month that had been used for payments allowed them to relax a little—until a few months later when another large contract came in. Again they hunkered down, cutting off all outflows and put the entire profit into their home. By the end of one year, they were completely debt-free. Through wisdom, they developed a strategy and now live in victory.

Every level of life is achieved incrementally. Debt, "smart leases" and "easy payment plans" will enslave you by increments. Celebrating the death of each debt will propel you into prosperity by increments. *Start with wisdom, develop a strategy, and you will see a victory.*

STEWARDSHIP

Your life can be summed up in three words: *stewardship, relationship, leadership.* You do not own what you possess. You are only the steward of it. You don't own your spouse's love, your children's affection, or your peers' respect. You are only the steward of them. Everything you have today is subject to change. And if you're a poor steward, it will change.

A famous pop singer thought she had achieved the pinnacle of her profession and could do whatever she wanted. She missed appearances, refused interviews, was rude to fans and demanded special services. Her career declined and she was eventually eclipsed, losing everything. A wife took advantage of her husband, didn't appreciate his talents or his work, and lost his love. A father never took time for his children, depended on hearing reports about them from his wife, and failed in his relationship with them. All are examples of poor stewardship.

Stewardship is key to every area of life, none more than our finances. One of the greatest errors we make in stewardship is in our giving. The principle is, "Givers gain." Suze Orman is a financial guru for millions. She teaches giving as a source of power and one of the means to achieve personal success. People follow her because they discover it's true. *Givers gain.*

"Give and it shall be given to you," is one of the most powerful proverbs you can ever commit to memory. You may think, *"As soon as I'm out of debt, I'll start giving."* Debt-free living allows you to give more, but if you never start giving, you'll never start getting. *You have to give before you can get.*

Emil and Julia are a great example. They launched out in business with a written plan and a set of goals. They took out a small loan and attended training to launch their new enterprise. Privately, they made a decision to give based on their goals, not their income. At first, their level of giving depressed their level of living, but they stuck with their strategy. At the end of the first year, they had met their financial goals and were ready to set more. They increased their goals, and their giving each year, and before long they paid off their loans and prospered. Giving caused them to gain.

HOW AND WHERE TO GIVE

People stumble over giving because they worry about how the money will be used. As with any investment, you must learn about the organization or people to whom you are giving before you make the gift. But once it's made, let it go. If you truly give, you won't worry about what they do with it.

Two easy principles will help you decide how to give. The first is, give away from yourself. If your company has its own charity that you control, that's a great and noble work, but don't make that your only avenue of giving. Put some money out of your own control by giving to others. Second, take care of your family.

I told you about John who changed careers and prospered after making a change in the way he handled money. The change was so simple, its results are astonishing. He was giving to his local church, and felt he was doing his duty, but he read one evening that you should take care of your own family before increasing your giving to others, even to God. John and his wife talked it over and agreed to send a check to his parents. Months passed and their finances increased so they could send a check to her parents as well. Over the years they have been able to give hundreds of times more than they gave in the beginning, and they have steadfastly followed the principle that unlocked the power of prosperity in the first place.

Hector's story was slightly different. Hector heard John's story and realized that he'd never truly given to his impoverished mother. Remember, this was a woman who had been kicked out of tenements her entire adult life. Trying to be a good son, Hector had bought her things to alleviate her circumstances, but he'd never just given her money. She had always felt the rejection from when he left her in his childhood, and she had always felt his control when he returned now to help her. Hector changed that and started sending checks with no strings attached. He didn't hear from her at first, but slowly she came around. Today they have a truly prosperous relationship for the first time in their lives.

Remember that love is the desire to benefit others, even at your own expense. A greater sorrow than a person not seeing a need, is the person who sees it and can do nothing about it. But a greater sorrow still is the person who sees the need, can do something about it, but doesn't.

Two things always make people happy: receiving a gift from someone and giving to someone. You can only control one of those two things, so exercise your power of choice and give! Largeness of heart allows for enlarging your business.

The San Diego Padres, McDonald's and Target stores are all examples of companies that have learned to give. By giving to the community, they build relationships and ties with their constituents that could not come by any other means. After the Los Angeles riots, the McDonald's franchises were among the first to reopen their doors because they suffered the least damage. Why? Because the community felt connected to them through their gifts of after-school programs and other local aid.

Give through your hospitality. Give to the poor. Give to your family. Give to widows. Give food to starving nations. Give to those who teach you. Set a portion of your money aside and just give!

What Givers Gain

Your care for others is the measure of your greatness. People try to be great *at* something, not realizing greatness is measured by serving. What made American carmakers great for years was the number of customers they served. Dell Computers was not great until their customer service was noticed and their customer base increased. Caring for others made them great.

You gain by giving what you cannot buy with money. Money cannot buy you greatness, respect, prosperity or well-being. But by giving you can gain all four.

Jamal's business outgrew his facilities, and the working conditions became cramped. Jamal was a giver, and even though he had a need on which he wanted to consume all his resources, he continued instead to give. A large office building had been standing vacant for some years. Jamal occasionally drove by and finally saw a sign from a leasing agency that was trying to retrofit the building to serve as executive offices. When Jamal went to the leasing agents, they were anxious for his business because they needed someone to occupy part of the building to prime the pump for more business.

He knew he couldn't afford luxury offices like the ones they talked about, so Jamal went home. The image of that building haunted him, so Jamal sat down and made a list of what he considered to be the sun, moon and stars: a total of 27 demands he required to move in. One was free rent for a specified period of time. Going back on a follow-up call, he gave them the list and was startled when they didn't blink. They gave him every demand. Jamal gained by giving what he could not control nor buy with money.

THE TRICK TO RECEIVING

"It is more blessed to give than to receive," is widely quoted but routinely misunderstood. Giving leads to receiving. So if you give *and* receive, both together are more blessed than merely receiving. But receiving is a trick in itself.

Don set out after college with an aim to become poor. He believed that rich people were bad and poor people were good, and he wanted to be good, so he wanted to be poor. He gave away whatever he received, but whenever he did, more came. Finally Don took his young bride to another country to help impoverished people, but even there, he could not escape from things falling into his lap. Eventually it occurred to him that if he had something to give, he could help more people than if he had nothing, so he started accepting what was given to him. Don corrected his poverty mentality and became a millionaire many times over, but he never strayed far from the principles that brought him his wealth, and he is still today one of the most generous people I know.

Don stumbled upon two principles. One: givers gain. Secondly: receiving is as important as believing. You can exercise faith and believe for your dreams to come true, but if you are unable or unwilling to receive the means by which they come true, you'll never succeed. Once Don received what was given to him, he became prosperous.

Receiving is as important as believing.

Answers for your needs will always come through people. Refusing the people, or being too proud to accept their help, sabotages success. Who can forget the characters in Jane Austen's famous novel, *Pride and Prejudice*, who kept missing opportunities for romance. Because they prejudged how love would come, and were too proud to accept the way it did come, they missed out. Once they overcame their prejudice and swallowed their pride, they succeeded. It will be the same for you when you learn to receive, and accept that your answers will come through people.

ENDOWED TO PROSPER!

If you are faithful in little, you will be faithful with much. You qualify for more by how you deal with less. If you are not faithful where you are, you cannot go beyond where you are.

A corollary principle is that if you are faithful in that which belongs to another, you qualify to have that which is your own. The business owner who is faithful to serve her first customers will find herself soon serving many customers.

By her faithfulness in the small numbers, she becomes qualified for large numbers. People who want to launch their own businesses, but are unfaithful while working for others, disqualify themselves for success in their own company. The saying is, "what goes around comes around." The proverb is, "You reap what you sow." Say it how you want, it's true.

Let's assume you are already faithful. What comes next? Investing. Prospering financially doesn't come down to how much you save or waste, but to how much you invest. The principle of investing is that *by use you possess and gain, by disuse you decline and lose.*

My son-in-law Richard works out regularly and disciplines himself to keep fit, far above most men his age. But if Richard were to get his body where he wanted it, then protected it by staying indoors, covering it with a robe, hiding it so it wouldn't get ruined, he would lose everything he had earned in the gym. On the other hand, if he continues to use it, he'll gain even more. *It's the same with money.*

Use it and you will gain from it. It's true of love, faith, your body, every virtue, and even money. Colloquially we say, "Use it or lose it." Divine math began in the Garden of Eden with a command to Adam to multiply. Math for the purpose of growth and increase is not addition but multiplication. You add by saving, but you multiply by investing. Investing is simply gaining by trading. Putting your money to use is its best use.

H. Ross Perot once claimed that he didn't have a dollar that wasn't working for him. When you consider his fortune, it's a claim that is impossible not to believe. You gain by saving, but multiply by investing.

These principles will guide you in your investments:

1. *Invest in people.* When you invest, you never invest in a company, corporation or business, but always in the person running it. Investing is personal. You invest in the person. Find out who runs the company before investing either your life or your money in it. Con artists influence people to invest based on those who have invested, never by selling themselves to the investor. People put faith in other investors, but the company collapses because of the man running it. That's who you're investing in.

2. *Before investing, investigate.*

3. *Risk, don't gamble.*

4. *It must be in writing.* I knew two men who were partners for over twenty-five years and never had a disagreement because everything they did they wrote down. Take the time to write it down.

5. *Don't live with death.* If you lose an investment, bury it.

6. *Invest in producers.* First class managers hire first class people. Second class managers hire third class people. Go first class. Go with those who produce.

7. *Shadows are more fierce than reality.* Don't avoid reality because you're afraid of what you might find. Cast a spotlight on murky shadows and find the truth.

8. *Funds come from friends*. Be concerned about making friends, not just clients or customers.

9. *Invest your life for your greatest good*. Any investment you make is always an investment of yourself.

10. *Don't quit.*

When it comes to money, you have to start somewhere. You'll never experience financial freedom until you learn to live without debt. But you'll never be free from debt until you learn to give. Be faithful, then start to invest. The principle is, you sow to the future, and reap from the past. Make your future bright today by setting the patterns in motion.

- Too many people buy things they don't need with money they don't have to impress people they don't like.

- The use of your money reveals more about your character than anything else.

- How you spend your money shows what you do with your life.

- Master the principles that master money.

- If you don't work, you don't eat.

- Money follows ministry.

- Financial poverty springs from spiritual poverty in the heart.

- Loving money ensures you'll never have money enough.

- Prosperity is first in heart, then in finances.

- Debt has become a modern form of slavery.

- Temptations to do wrong always promise on the surface to serve and please but only desire to enslave and dominate.

- People are negative by nature and have to be converted to the positive.

- Every level of life is achieved incrementally.

- Start with wisdom, develop a strategy, and you will see a victory.

- Your life can be summed up in three words: stewardship, relationship, leadership.

- You do not own what you possess. You are only the steward of it.

- Givers gain.

- Give and it shall be given to you.

- You have to give before you can get.

- Give away from yourself.

- A greater sorrow than a person not seeing a need, is the person who sees it and can do nothing about it. But a greater sorrow still is the person who sees the need, can do something about it, but doesn't.

- Largeness of heart allows for enlarging your business.

- Your care for others is the measure of your greatness.

- You gain by giving what you cannot buy with money.

- Receiving is as important as believing.
- Answers for your needs will always come through people.
- If you are faithful with little, you will be faithful with much.
- If you are faithful in that which belongs to another, you qualify to have that which is your own.
- You reap what you sow.
- Investing is simply gaining by trading.
- By use you possess and gain, by disuse you decline and lose.
- Use it or lose it.
- You add by saving, but multiply by investing.
- When you invest, you never invest in a company, corporation or business, but always in the person running it.
- You sow to the future, and reap from the past.

CHAPTER SIX

MAINTAIN WHAT YOU OBTAIN

Fame can come in a moment, but greatness comes with longevity. Some of the greatest athletes, politicians, musicians, entertainers, educators, scientists and leaders in our country have suffered collapse—men and women who were revered and lauded in their moment of fame. How can you avoid their fate?

Three major requisites for success are: *Plan wisely, use common sense, and be strong in what you know is right.* Get help from others for any of these three.

Counselors determine the destiny of kings. In bygone days, before kings went to war, they always sought counsel. One ancient king sought counsel from people who had worked with his father and knew what made success. He also consulted those who came to power when he did, and who were seeking positions in the kingdom. They gave their advice not based on what was good for the king, but what was good for them. The king took their advice, and he split the nation, losing the major part of it.

A common weakness in people is thinking that others are always right or smarter. They are not. "They" can be dangerous if listened to without understanding. Seek counsel, advice and wisdom, but be sure to find out what "they" have done, how "they" have done it and what "they" have learned. There is safety in many counselors, especially those who have been where you are and learned what you need to know.

When you allow people to influence your choices, you must know their pedigree. Not everything people say to you deserves to be heard. If they don't have your welfare in mind, their words can poison your thinking, particularly if what they say is negative in nature. Shut them up, or their words may shut you down. Taking time to listen shows respect for others. Listening to foolish people shows disrespect for self.

You're never too old to seek counsel. "Better is a poor and wise youth than an old and foolish king who no longer knows how to receive counsel," states Solomon's proverb. Thinking we know everything is the start of our demise.

RELATIONSHIPS

I said earlier your life can be summed up in three words: stewardship, relationship, leadership. We talked about stewardship, but let's look at relationship. Communication is the basis for relationship. If we don't communicate, we can't relate.

Ronald Reagan was dubbed "The Great Communicator." Political experts said President Clinton's abilities even surpassed Reagan's. Reagan was dubbed the "Teflon" president because of the way he deflected criticism, and Clinton was named the "Comeback Kid" for his many comebacks after his tremendous failures. Even with ideologies miles apart, their communication skills enabled individuals to relate to them and both became two-term presidents. Both communicated that they were listening to the American public and acting in the people's best interest.

Listening is the basic art of communication. You don't make a success in life by your ability to speak, but by your ability to listen. The world's poorest salespeople always talk past the point of the sale. The more words we speak, the less they mean. Remember the legendary insurance salesman? He perfected the art of selling by perfecting the art of listening.

The art of communication is not based on speaking but on listening. Prosperity and success are not based on what you say but what you hear. Listening has the power of healing. An irresistible man for a woman is the man who is a good listener. Children likewise are frustrated when Mom and Dad haven't time to listen. The three common areas that hinder prospering in a family are communication, sex and money.

The formula for success in real estate is "location, location, location." The formula for success in relationships, including business and family, is "communication, communication, communication." *If we don't communicate, we can't relate.*

Reliable communication allows for progress. Unreliable information causes the whole system to suffer.

Learn to relate by learning to listen. Relationships precede success in business. But don't let your workplace become your hiding place. Go home and relate as well. No one ever said on his deathbed his only regret was not spending more time at the office.

Stewardship, relationship, leadership.

LEADERSHIP

The purpose of leadership is to influence. *Leaders determine to influence, followers only happen to.* Three foundations exist upon which to build leadership skills: character, integrity and influence. We do not influence industries or nations, we only influence people.

Influence is one of the most precious commodities in life. It is wise to use but criminal to sell. More money is spent on influence than any other commodity—political campaigns, lobbying, media, religion, to name a few.

As a leader, you must choose employees whom you will lead by influence, and they must meet one basic criteria: faithfulness. Faithfulness is the cornerstone of character. Remember the two employees? The first was often absent and always late. The second was less talented, but faithfully there. You can commit major projects to the second, not the first because you can commit to character, not to talent.

Transposition is the common error of life. We transpose letters on the keyboard to create "untie" instead of "unite." We also transpose talent and character. We commit to the talented instead of the faithful, to our own hurt.

Three ingredients comprise faithfulness: *constancy, loyalty, and submission.* Constancy means never varying, steadfast. Loyal are those who are firmly attached, who would never disclose a confidence and are quick to stand up for the cause. "Leaks" come from those loyal only to their own agenda. Submission is simply the willingness to subject yourself to another.

To attract personnel with character, be a leader with character. Remember, you reap what you sow. There's also a principle that says, "*The characteristics of the kingdom emanate from the character of the king.*" What is within your own heart will show up in your business, and in your family.

A publishing house in California is known for taking care of the people they do business with, from big-name authors to free-lance proofreaders. When a member of the staff says they'll call you back, they call you back. Their courtesy and professional manner reflects well on the owner, and gives outsiders a glimpse into the owner's heart. In no way could a company like that spring from selfish, miserly ownership. That owner's influence shows up in every employee, down to the beginning clerk.

Personnel is always the problem and personnel is always the solution. Finding and training people is a lifelong duty if you intend to be successful. The basic pattern for management is—*win them, train them, send them.* It's the same in sports, customer service, restaurants, churches, and it's the same for parents.

Disneyland's strategy is to train new hires in the parking area for days before unleashing them, because those are the first people the public encounters. They would seem to have the easiest job, yet they receive some of the best training.

When training, remember that people don't do what you expect, but what you inspect. You can teach the best plan, but if you never check up, they may never work your plan. Train them, give them responsibility, and have them account for it.

Responsibility without accountability is an error. You cannot hold someone accountable for something for which they were not responsible.

The unfaithful employee is mediocre and wants authority, not accountability. A faithful employee grows in responsibility because they are willing to be held accountable.

THE QUIET POISON

The opposite of a faithful employee is not necessarily lazy or sloppy, but seditious. Sedition is the undermining of constituted authority with the attempt to overthrow it. Sedition is listed in the Bible with sins such as witchcraft and hatred because it is such a virulent poison.

Sedition is an act of treason, punishable by law. Those who commit treason in our government are treated as traitors and can even be sentenced to death. It is one of the most unrecognized and destructive forces in human nature. Those who engage in destruction cause their own destruction. The proverb says, "He who sows the wind will reap the whirlwind." Unfortunately, a whirlwind takes everyone around it down with it.

In the home, sedition is seen when the son asks Mom for a dollar. She says, "You've already spent your dollar this week and you can't have another one." So he goes to his father and asks him. This is human nature. But, if that father says, "Mom won't give you a dollar? I'll give you one," he is committing an act of sedition, undermining his wife's authority over their child.

On the job, sedition is the secretary being given a job to do and quickly emailing the other secretary to tell how unfair it is, and how they should both quit to hurt the boss. Or the salesman standing around the water cooler, waiting for people to walk by whom he can poison with his complaints about how he can't sell because management won't give him any freedom. Learn to recognize and wipe out sedition!

THE RIGHT TIME

Let's say you've mastered these principles, built a good character, hired a terrific staff, but still you don't quite break through. What's the problem? Timing.

Success comes from being the right person, at the right time in the right place. *Timing is the essential ingredient in success.*

Everything in life is seasonal. We can't change the seasons, we can only adapt to them. Time, like fruit, ripens. Fruit spoils if picked too late and is sour if picked too early.

Henry Ford built cars before there were roads on which to drive them. He influenced decision-makers to speed up the timing for the roads or he wouldn't have had a marketable product.

When people have had a brush with death is a great time to sell them life insurance. When they're planning their daughter's wedding is not the best time to sell them a car. It's all timing.

Life management begins with time management. Time is the great equalizer because all people are given the same twenty-four hours in a day. We cannot save time. We can only use it effectively. We have no second chance to live today.

THE NATURE OF TIME

The nature of time is—past, present, future. At the beginning, all time is future. Time comes out of the future and flows into the past. Tomorrow will soon be today, then yesterday. That is the unbroken order of the motion of time.

Human history flows from out of the past into the present, but time flows from out of the future. We do not flow with time. We continually meet it instant by instant. Time and humanity meet in the present. That means, today is the only day you have. The past is irretrievable and there is no tomorrow, for when it comes, it will be today.

We learn from the past to do in the present what will provide for the future. The future is the reservoir from which life comes. The future is unseen, unknown, except as it makes itself visible in the present. The present embodies the future then returns again to the past. The past acts invisibly to influence us and cast light upon the present with reference to the future.

Time is worthy of respect. To procrastinate is to disrespect time. Procrastinators live under self-induced stress, and at the mercy of those who respect time. To waste time is also to disrespect time. *Not every demand is worthy of our time, just as not every word spoken is worthy to be heard.*

I remember a story about Winston Churchill demanding a subordinate to produce a report. The first time it was submitted, Churchill met with the subordinate and told him the report was rejected. The second time, he again rejected it. The third time, the subordinate wiped the sweat off his brow as he stood at Churchill's desk and said, "I'm sorry, Sir, but I don't believe I can do any better than this."

"Okay," Churchill said, "this time I'll read it."

We must discipline ourselves to respect our own time. To organize is to show respect. Organizing time shows respect for time. People who fail to organize their personal, familial or professional lives show disrespect for their own lives and for those with whom they have relationship.

Organization brings peace, whereas disorganization brings conflict, discord and disharmony. Symphonies are comprised of notes and sounds organized in arrangements to create harmony. Harmony is comprised of sounds played in respect, one for another, by people who are respectful one of another. Musicians playing in an orchestra show respect for music, people, and purpose by submitting to one another in the use of time and talent. Harmony in the family, the business, and within yourself is as sweet as a melodious symphony.

We never "find time" but must "make time" for the important. It was A. R. Bernard again who said, "We stifle creativity by spending too much time on maintenance." To concentrate on maintenance instead of creatively addressing your competition will cause you to lose your place in the market.

Success is not based on the ability to say yes, but the ability to say no. Resisting the extraneous, illegitimate, and unnecessary, allows for occupation with the productive, positive, and vital.

When time exists it is forever, but it comes to us from its source in the future—the next century, decade, year, month, week, day—and then it is today. *Today has the possibility of eternal good in it, depending on how you use it.*

Money and time are both means to an end, not an end in themselves. They are resources, not goals. But it takes a combination of time and money to reach our goals.

OVERCOMING BARRIERS

Tomorrow has never seen a failure. Any failure that comes today will soon be yesterday. Yesterday's dung is tomorrow's fertilizer.

It was Og Mandino who wrote that only the inferior are always at their best. Crises, setbacks and occasional failures occur for everyone, but they cannot in and of themselves hurt you. Problems drive out the worst in you, and bring out the best in you. The difference between people who fail and those who succeed often lies in how they handle the pressure of adversity.

Colonel Sanders slept in the back seat of his car as he drove to hundreds of restaurants looking for one that would try his recipe for chicken. With each "no," he was one restaurant closer to the one that would say "yes."

Failure is the womb of success. Success is born out of failure. Successful people like Colonel Sanders do not fear failure, because each failure brings them closer to success. *The successful don't live with failure. They bury it.*

Fear of failure is the only sure way to live with it. Like the widow who wouldn't dispose of her husband's things, you cannot afford to live with death. Don't carry past mistakes around like a dead carcass. As long as you talk about them, they live.

In front of every promise there is a problem. If you only look at the problem, you will lose sight of the promise. John Maxwell says, "Winners look at what they're going to, losers look at what they're going through." Everyone has to put up with stuff, but being able to overcome it is the difference between those who achieve excellence and those who wallow in the morass of mediocrity.

The great All-Pro defensive lineman Reggie White was on a college football team ranked ninetieth for defense. It was an embarrassment. He had the promise of being a great defensive player, but he had a problem in that his defensive squad stunk. What he did about it was simply go to the gym and work harder. He didn't condemn the other guys. He just lifted his own level of play. After he improved, his teammates began to hit the gym as well, and they rose from ninetieth to ninth in one season.

To improve your life, work on yourself. It does nothing to complain about others. People love to complain and find fault with others—their spouses, children, employers, employees, upline, downline, trainer, trainees, recruiter, inductees—for themselves feeling unfulfilled, unhappy, discontented and restless. What good will it do? None.

In a meeting recently I was with people who had been bankrupt, were retired bus drivers, overworked executives facing downsizing—and they were also all millionaires. Each had overcome adversity to achieve new heights. Ever had a failure? Great, you qualify to succeed! Some man came to me one day all distraught and complained, "I lost a million dollars."

"Great," I said, "then you know how to make a million—so go out and do it again!"

Success is the greatest antidote to failure. If you want to get over failing—be successful! But if you want to complain about your failure and find others on whom to blame it, you'll live with that failure for life.

Maturity does not come with age but begins with the acceptance of responsibility. Responsibility for success is built upon being responsible for failure. Generally the person who is afraid to fail is also the one who cannot handle success.

All success is born out of failure. If you never quit, you cannot fail. Failure is not the worst thing in the world—quitting is. Champions are not those who never fail, but those who never quit. *Stay in 'til you win*!

FINAL WORDS

Always remember to build your business before building your own salary, bank account or personal possessions. Profits are the lifeblood of any economy. Profits establish where the heart is. It is easy to put your heart into something that will provide your livelihood, care for your family, and give you something to invest.

Hard work brings prosperity; playing around brings poverty. You can always tell the manager or owner by the way they pick up, put away, straighten, or rearrange things that are open to the gaze of the public. They see what the paid worker fails to see and that is why they are the boss. *Do the work of the boss and one day you'll be one.*

And regardless of what comes your way, remember that above the clouds, the sun always shines. Keep going, the clouds will soon be gone. The sun is shining bright for you!

- Fame can come in a moment, but greatness comes with longevity.

- Counselors determine the destiny of kings.

- Taking time to listen shows respect for others. Listening to foolish people shows disrespect for self.

- Better is a poor and wise youth than an old and foolish king who no longer knows how to receive counsel.

- Communication is the basis for relationship.

- If we don't communicate, we can't relate.

- Listening is the basic art of communication.

- You don't make a success in life by your ability to speak but by your ability to listen.

- The three common problem areas in a family are communication, sex and money.

- Reliable communication allows for progress.

- Relationships precede success.

- Don't let your workplace become your hiding place.

- No one ever said on his deathbed his only regret was not spending more time at the office.

- Influence is one of the most precious commodities in life.

- Faithfulness is the cornerstone of character.

- You can commit to character, not to talent.

- The characteristics of the kingdom emanate from the character of the king.

- Personnel is always the problem and personnel is always the solution.

- The basic pattern for management is—win them, train them, send them.

- People don't do what you expect, but what you inspect.

- You cannot hold someone accountable for something for which they were not responsible.

- Success comes from being the right person, at the right time in the right place.

- Timing is the essential ingredient in success.

- We can't change the seasons, we can only adapt to them.

- Life management begins with time management.

- Time is the great equalizer because everyone is given the same twenty-four hours in a day.

- Today is the only day you have.

- To procrastinate or to waste time is to disrespect time. Organizing time shows respect for time.

- Not every demand is worthy of our time, just as not every word spoken is worthy to be heard.

- We never "find time" but must "make time" for the important.

- We stifle creativity by spending too much time on maintenance.

- Success is not based on the ability to say yes, but the ability to say no.

- Today has the possibility of eternal good in it, depending on how you use it.

- Yesterday's dung is tomorrow's fertilizer.

- Only the inferior are always at their best.

- Problems drive out the worst in you, and bring out the best in you.

- The difference between people who fail and those who succeed often lies in how they handle the pressure of adversity.

- Failure is the womb of success.

- Fear of failure is the only sure way to live with it.

- In front of every promise there is a problem. If you only look at the problem, you will lose sight of the promise.

- Winners look at what they're going to, losers look at what they're going through.

- Success is the greatest antidote to failure. If you want to get over failing—be successful!

- Maturity does not come with age but begins with the acceptance of responsibility.

- Responsibility for success is built upon being responsible for failure.

- All success is born out of failure.
- If you never quit, you cannot fail.
- Failure is not the worst thing in the world—quitting is.
- Champions are not those who never fail, but those who never quit.
- Stay in 'til you win!
- Hard work brings prosperity; playing around brings poverty.
- Above the clouds the sun always shines.
- The sun is shining bright for you!

EPILOGUE

This epilogue is free. The cost of the book did not include this page, so reading it is entirely optional.

The only reason for an epilogue is that I cannot in good conscience give readers the impression that the material in this book is my own. My mind is not the mind that conceived these patterns and principles, nor did I discover them on my own without help.

Patterns and principles were set in motion from the beginning of the universe by a Creator God. They are His. The only thing people can do is discover and acknowledge them, ignore them, or pervert them. Perverted principles lead to perverse living. Living by principle causes people to prosper, families to flourish, and nations to be upheld.

The ultimate standards of human behavior and rules for conduct are found in the words of the Creator God, the Holy Bible. This is more than opinion. It is my personal belief, upon which I've based seventy-plus years of life and my future eternity. You are free to form your own opinion. I'm just older than you, so I give you the benefit of my years.

The world's greatest handbook for learning economic basics is not a textbook, but a Bible.

We are all free today to choose the way we live because we were given free choice at the point of creation. Our freedom of choice is the only true freedom we have. We can choose even to ignore this power and live as if we have no choices.

The greatest choice a person will make in this world is what they will do when they leave it. A passage from the

Book of Ecclesiastes reads, "A wise man thinks much of death, while the fool thinks only of having a good time now" (Ecclesiastes 7:4, *The Living Bible*).

The principle is, "the first in intention is the last in execution." When we plan a sales event, the ultimate result is to have customers, so we must plan what we want to do with those customers in order to determine the best kind of event and how to conduct it. In the same way, when we plan our lives, we must look to what we want after life is over to determine what life we choose and how we conduct it.

I believe the Bible leads us to right choices, good patterns and sound principles. If you have never read it, I encourage you to invest in a Bible today. Read it, then learn to live it.

If you need information about the Bible or need other help, call me at 1-800-225-6263, or write to me:

Ed Cole
P.O. Box 10
Grapevine, TX 76099
USA

NANCY CORBETT COLE CHARITIES

A portion of the proceeds from this book will be given to Nancy Corbett Cole Charities, serving the abused, addicted and abandoned. Internationally, "Nancy Corbett Cole Homes of Refuge" provide housing, vocational training and education for abused women and children. In the United States, help is ongoing on an individual and corporate basis.

Nancy Corbett Cole, "The Loveliest Lady in the Land," supported her husband, Edwin Louis Cole, in pursuing his life's mission for 54 years. Behind the scenes, she was a spiritual anchor and provider for many. Before her death in December, 2000, Nancy asked for the assurance that those for whom she had provided would not feel her absence. To fulfill that end, and for that purpose, Nancy Corbett Cole Charities were established.

By purchasing this book, you have already helped society's under-served and less privileged members. If this book helped you, please consider sending a generous donation as well. Your one-time or continual support will help the helpless, heal the hurting, and relieve the needy. Your gift is fully tax-deductible in the U.S. Send your compassionate contribution to:

Nancy Corbett Cole Charities
P.O. Box 92501
Southlake, TX 76092
USA

Thank you for your cheerful and unselfish care for others.

Watch for more Watercolor Books™

by terrific authors like:

Edwin Louis Cole
Nancy Corbett Cole
Donald Ostrom

Many more!

www.watercolorbooks.com

For international orders
or publishing, contact
Access Sales International
www.access-sales.com
or
dianae@access-sales.com

Also by Edwin Louis Cole

Maximized Manhood
Potential Principle
Real Man
Strong Men in Tough Times
ManPower
Absolute Answers to Prodigal Problems
COURAGE
Communication, Sex & Money
*Winners Are Not Those Who Never Fail,
but Those Who Never Quit*
Unique Woman
Irresistible Husband